INLAND

EMPIRE

poems

LEAH HUIZAR

INLAND
EMPIRE

poems

LEAH HUIZAR

INLAND EMPIRE

HOMINY

Consider *menudo*—a word like *mundo* which suggests a world,
or, in this bowl, many spinning bodies. Intestines float

over heaps of hominy anchored in chile broth and citrus
squeeze. We eat. Sundays in San Diego taquerias

the patter and heave of slurping on slippery organs
rises in a sung homiletic. My father tells me of a place

deep in Mexico's belly where everyone looks like us—hard tuft
eyebrows like slabs of meat heavily cut, the kind

made soft over heat, over time. Oh, infinitely variable
Mexican supper of substitution: trade honeycomb

tripe for *carnitas*—the diminutive flesh, the affectionate *-ita*,
as in *cariñita*, little loved one (if love were feminine), little brown

bouquets cinched by a rub of fat. In California's Inland Empire,
my aunt's stove hums a drum-pot of soup, an incantation

older than the New World, a pre-Columbian stock bubbling at lips
lately made. In Mesoamerican myth, man was created

three times. The mud of earth made man mute and motionless;
wood turned him forgetful and soulless. Only the pliant

dough of two types of cornmeal could shape the knots and joints,
the new formed limbs of this human flesh.

PART I

"There ruled on that island of California, a queen great of body, very beautiful for her race, at a flourishing age, desirous in her thoughts of achieving great things, valiant in strength, cunning in her brave heart, more than any other who had ruled that kingdom before her...Queen Calafia."

— *Las Sergas de Esplandián*, Garci Rodríguez de Montalvo

SANTA ANA

They came with names like prayers, sweeping
and incantatory: Jose Antonio Yorba, Juan

Pablo Peralta. They came before the Declaration,
before figures become manifest against the Eastern

horizon, rolling out West, sick and determined. Chronicles
beyond what school books have asked us to imagine.

Their ranchos spread from water to water, edge
of the Santa Ana river to the wide embrace of the Pacific.

To hear these names as other than relics—namesake
streets and roads, architects of adobes—

means traveling to the pivot of hands
holding claim. The tribal nations living within

the sixty thousand acre tract lost first
to the missions, the grants, the measles, the hogs

that ate a hogs-share of native protein, acorns:
this, after the land grants came. Then, it turned

again. Domingo de la Resurrección sold his adobe,
El Refugio, to Jose Andres Sepulveda's family. This refuge,

however, failed its title and the Americans
came, post-1848, wanting proof of land claims. So came

the court cases, interest rates, mortgage
hikes. So came the wet years, the drought years,

the years the bones of a thousand cattle dry
on the Santa Ana hills. Then new names:

Bixby, Irvine, Flint. Spurgeon came to build
a western town upon the rancho's pasture. He settled

with new grids, and chose the same name: Santa Ana,
Mother of Mary, the double Madonna. Stage of many

dominions. Siren followed into both nest
and snare. More came. They came and came, men

with God-names and hard names.
They came to the hills that blaze and moan

with earthquakes, fires, and crumbling
mud homes. They came to the place that would

claim their bones. The past we map over land
and skin and will call by name.

CALAFIA

I.

Queen Calafia guards the corpus
California, woman and
land. She ascends
over this place of legend
once stretched just beyond
the known world. Here

lies the isle of paradise
where women with burnished
bodies in gilded armor
rule its abundance. Mountains
curve into valleys. Silt
slopes into rivers. The air
glows as sunlight
elides seawater swells and heat
simmer ripples over plains
of the chaparral. She gives

a name to the burning mirage on water.
Her myth becomes our flesh and walks
among us, as any other dream-past.

Calafia, Mother of all this gold:
See me, kindling on the flinted coast,
then teach me to glide like a flame over water.

II.

Dark and splendid Eve, bear in me
all missing mothers, all far-off fathers, all
ship-sunk sagas and lore floating over these tidewaters,

a haze of history to build out the fable. As day
ebbs, I'll call Calafia to mind:

She disrobes her metal weight at a seaside stand
and keeps watch. Overhead,
a brown-winged bird lifts a fox
pup to its nest, becomes a momentary
chimera. In the broad panorama, above
this estate and spun in dust and spume,
cleaved of arroyos, ranges, and woods,
she skims brightly the loam of the land,
California.

LA VIRGEN DE GUADALUPE

I. *Juan Diego's Apron*

Capture a Spanish rose
before it lands beside his feet:

Unrolled, rose heads cascade in the release.
The garment's woven image bears the brown

Madonna, belly swollen with a hybrid. If
this is conquest, then yes the heart

submits to follow her, as Joseph did
once, over other deserts, in winter.

II. *Empress of Latin America*

Legend lopes between historia y cuento
as my grandmother unspools

centuries of Mexican memory: She appeared as just
a woman on a lonely road. Not above deceit,

her words misdirected a roving army,
saved an outnumbered village.

On our drive up Oceanside's El Camino,
twisted rails open to ditch and field—

a white cross, a picture, plastic flowers—
a host of her prayer candles

band into a crash site's makeshift
shrine. She'll reign on roads, on cluttered

mantels, in split hearts,
a candle and its unburnt wick.

III. *The Brown Madonna*

They named her: "Little dark one."
Darkness of a sacred mother or mystery. Abuelita
turning tortillas at the metal comal.
Amazonian woman on a cliff, the breath of myth
blowing over sea monster maps, the medieval
Spanish ships searching the shore. Woman ineffable.

See the darkest woman there.

See.

Her hands are full.

Her hands are full and dark.

Her hands and lap are full.

Her child's face is full of darkness too.

My face is full of darkness.

ESCONDIDO

In 1983, my mother wept through winter.
Her body could not forget the sea salt

saturating morning's early breath,
piquant and thick with the harbor's

seaweed pungency. Fifteen miles
inland, she wheezes awake in the arid

valley that cradled my parents' first
apartment off Ash. This move, made

for love, folded her body in on itself, curled
at the round of her widening hips. She sank

beneath thin air, so unlike the mist
that poured into her Oceanside windows.

It could never quench her acute thirst. Night
brought other losses: the way salt dissolved into sleep

and lifted each unremembered dream
like buoys guided by the tide. Only

I—already inside, soaked in brine, floating
in the pit of her—could conjure that salt again. I
swirled and formed in her tremble and recoil.

ANCIENT AMERICAN SITE
—Moundville Archeological Park, Alabama

Centuries back something collapsed
here. Away from home, I tour the deep past
by tracing the park to its edges.
Beyond the bases of long-abandoned,
brassy mounds, the encircling
woods squat. I go in search for some preserved
wilderness but find sagging caution
tape wound around two trees at the trailhead,
and a "Temporarily Closed" sign toppled.
The green air presses down with new warm
rain. Mist drifts low and obscuring. I step
onward toward the marked-off path,
skid on scattered acorns. Old seeds rupture
where I tread. Among all that will remain
unrecorded, tell me what nature compelled
me beyond caution and into the fog,
certain I was not the first to trespass the signs.

GETTY GIFT SHOP MADONNA
—Giotto's Madonna and Child, ca. *1320-30*

Oh, kick-tender ribs that bore
out the bulk-bloom and violence

spun from the navel where new birth lines
stretch to form a jagged white rose.

The cross is years off, though you'll
clutch, like a son or a sin, the cruelty of loss.

Remember, how aloof he replied, "Who is my mother?"
while outside for him, your voice rose.

Teenage Madonna, not even a Joseph to love,
you squatted down in the water

and blood of Eve's first curse with nothing
to console but the guiding stars as they rose.

SANTA MONICA

In the Golden Age of carousels, Charles Looff set
pleasure piers down each coast through the Roaring

Twenties, the national diversion. Santa Monica's
Hippodrome upholds her promontory tip, a music box

sculpted eclectic in Byzantine, Californian and Moorish
lines. The carousel's horses swirl in circles. Each thick mane rides

the wind of perpetual motion. Their limbs rubbed into a buffed
shine. Marilyn Monroe lingered for weeks to watch the spinning;

she wore shades and a wig, and the conductor mentioned to her
she might get a job. Even today, passengers still cling to palominos

in spiraling races going nowhere but right where they are.
Brassy organs chime from above. Always, the light,

it streaks and blurs until the whole pier wades in billowing golden
haze. In that cloud, Santa Monicans float. The Ferris wheel revolves

like a water mill filling its buckets with sun. A few blocks inland,
pedestrians parade on Third Street's promenade:

psychic cats, soap-boxers, magicians and rave-light dancers
perform for the swarm of evening walkers strolling in bare legs

bronzed and chiseled in city shadow and light. When the Spanish
first landed on this bay, they christened and blessed and named

it for the day's feast, Saint Monica of Hippo. St. Augustine's
mother wept as he swirled through philosophies for living:

hedonist, neo-Platonist, Manichean. She awaited
the Western father's final conversion, believed

a bishop that it's not possible the son of all these tears
should perish. Unceasing, Santa Monica offers her name

to a city bathed in ocean water saltier than tears, her sons
and daughters in that golden light, turning and turning.

MANY CHANGES SHE SAYS TO ME, LITTLE BY LITTLE

Grandmother narrates each Camp Pendleton road we follow.
Near Lake O'Neil's entrance, it's 1968 again:
my mother scuttles toward the lake, runs to catch

my young uncles and aunts. Mother's street clothes
unroll from the towel and tumble behind her.
Uncle Carlos, healthy and alive, recovers

and holds them over his head; he cries, *Whose
big underwear?* Then plunging he disappears
beneath the green water. We pass the old hospital

lot, its building torn down and rebuilt for other purposes.
Grandmother must see the ward still, when she speaks of days
after she had my mother. She says, *The place of your mom,*

*I learn little by little the English. I tell
the white ladies the Spanish words; I say agua
to the pregnant girls, and they tell me—*

Here she turns from the road to my face, places
fist in palm as if to hand off this story, her words,
something solid. She says—*this is the water.*

WHY SEEK THE LIVING AMONG THE DEAD?

Reverberating, the quake woke me early. Scales uncommon
most everywhere but here, the rocking brought little
distress. Like Lazarus, I awoke and turned toward the domestic.

I moved house-check pacing through the room's slight shifts,
noted the stability of table and corner statue of St. Mary,
the flightiness of succulents and unboxed ornaments. I'd missed,

while sleeping, the gut-feeling of a coming rumble
rising up hill, missed a crank window unlatch
itself, and the crèche's hay shudder. Drought year

rain followed the morning's spasms and a curb-dumped Christmas
tree rolled in the yard's fresh mud. After this chance
opening of ground and sky, new shoots—root-loose

and out-of-time—will burst forth. They'll cling to the unsettled
surface before disappearing, all at once, in winter's sun.

COMMUNION

I. *The Body*

My daily bread comes corn-based,
Maseca masa made into
gorditas and tortillas.

When I was a child I ate flour
tortillas; now I put away such
things, join Mother and Grandmother's

appetite for dough that won't
roll out, dough that must be crushed
and pressed into dense wafers.

I grow powerful in oblation.
In consuming, I double.

II. *The Blood*

Lip-tipped face-shadowed
cup of the real blood:

we share a cup and
drink over the mouth of another.

Memory fills the chalice.
Do this in remembrance of me.

Memory, Jesus announces—
for the forgiveness of sins—

is the same act as absolution. We recall
so many lips.

III. *January at Epiphany*

Amid a naked wood and barren back acre,
the winter morning twitches. A few leaves

float from a kumquat tree, a slack branch
bounces on a bed of fallen fruits,

squashed grass surges and drops.
Sun sifts through shifting clouds. The mute

day yawns. A familiar cardinal—female
and so more brown than bright—

drinks her fill from a broken cup.

HARBOR DRIVE'S *STAR OF INDIA*

Like many, she began with another name, one of joy—
Eutrepe, the ancient muse of poetry and music.
In 1863, how that promise must have held

the ship's immigrants leaving the Isle of Man.
See them, hunkered under deck and in bilge,
swaying over the plumbless seas. Centuries

pass and the oldest, active sailing ship,
now *Star of India*, anchors off San Diego's harbor.
The thin line of Harbor Drive divides ship

dock and international airport. Mother
would bring us girls to the wharf. We'd eat packed
roast beef, listen to the shore's current, trace the planes

ascending and descending: seat of all possible
departure. The game was aspiration, imagination: *Why*
are they going? What brought them here? Where

would we *go*? Once, I went and stayed overnight
on the ship, seventh grade. I boarded
Star of India with classmates, a knapsack on my back, tin

bowl tied to my side. The mates versed me in scurvy
and rope knots. The captain made me, for history's sake, a man;
he called me Mister—and with all that power, free

and unaccountable for anything but what my eyes
could see, I worked mast ropes and paced the deck
through the second shift of the night.

Years of plotted embarkment—I watched
the shore become a foreign place. Distant couples
bathed in midnight and gas lamp. Seaweed

surfed under the moon. The knotted
deck looked up, hazel like my father's eyes.
That night, a hundred and fifty years

overdue, for this green hand sailor traversing
the known world, I sang with *Eutrepe*,
her immigrants all buried, I hoped, on land.

LABOR

I. *Immigration*

She lived under leaves, lissome and cold,
in a wild bed burrowed beneath the arched roots
of a banyan tree. Time grew rings in the soles of her
feet. She wagered one forest for another kind and so left

the roots and the beetles, all she carved from dust.
She rode a winding path into backdoors left ajar. In these new
places, she swept the rooms of wooden
mistresses, embraced their linens. She scrubbed

their sheets. Her spine bent and unbent under
the wet mornings. Skin and cloth slogged up and
down against furrowed washboard ridges. Chipped knuckles
plunged into smoky water. She wrung out the days.

II. *Skins*

Here is how to skin potatoes, to get bone-
close like her: Flick the peeler's blade
a cut above a bracing thumb. Whittle
what's withered. Scalpel the sheath that rots.
Run down the starch bodies, separate
skins from cores. Rind soil will rub
into one's pores, wet, where fingers
glide. Cut again with a chef's knife,
incisions so clean the oval flats
glint like mirrors. The starch will bead
but don't stop. Cut and cut,
while the beige oxidized in air turns dark,
the way blood does on leaving the body.

MESSENGER

The messenger of God, a Mexican barber
by trade, taps the table with arthritic fingers.

You wouldn't understand… the woman tells him,
flitting cigarette embers on the marble tile,

…how hard… Her eyes—iridescent like a shell's
smooth side—follow the flutter of ash.

He looks up, says he recognizes her face,
asks for her last cigarette, then doesn't raise

it to his lips. He rolls it like dough in his palms—
How can I go…

the tobacco spilling out like leaves from a storm wrung tree.
He twists the empty zigzag into a stem, fans

out the filter, and hands back an American Spirit
flower. Tells her, she shouldn't bask in rote losses.

Look at him. He's content to work out
new pangs in the joints of these knuckles.

RENDERED MIRACLES

Emulsion of hand-beat cream starts to clump
into a butter-headed batter, while
the cribbed and crying baby sucks a plastic
ring.
       Woman, are you unhappy?
Did I see it in your recent cake? Lumps
that were not sifted. Still, here you stand,
move to steal the wet ring from the child,
chide quiet, go back to the business
of butter—
       your forearm burns from rapid whisking
around of thick, raw cream. Little flecks
of foam fling from your bowl to mar the gold
drapes, wood floors.
       If you just keep working this
fat from milk, whip and whip it past
froth and foam, until the moment, like a
miracle, when whatever it was—that
one cup of cream—splits and the buttermilk
spills forth from sudden forming blondish balls
of butter,
       then girl, if you can draw
a solid from such a silken liquid
thing, fracture the fats, break, beat them apart
into smallest matter that will remold
itself a hardened mass, then you are not
so finger-trapped, weak-armed, as you conceived.

BETWEEN

Bundles of baby's-breath lay at the florist's stall—frail
piles of white tufts like cells from lungs. In weddings,

they tangle in hair, hazard of araneous stems.
A couple holds a bouquet. Bent, as one,

they inhale in resuscitative pulses to draw new
scent from the dry buds. I've done this too,

in houses dense with dead skin motes, the body
becoming air. I am the hand that moves

between breaths, kith of doctors and priests.
I arrange wreaths, and hold remnant

dander on my tongue, tuck them in my diaphragm,
against the spine, pull specks of pungency

inside. In the gardens of heaven, no one marries
and no one dies. And here already,

aromas rent from what we put to our lips;
breath for breath, what's taken in persists. I enter

gatherings and see by window light my figure.
If I exhale, I seed the room.

COLLECTION

As a girl, I thought stones
spoke in ciphers. I read
them all over.

Pyrite was fixed as the burning bush,
a fire up hill.

Obsidian broke as an egg
in half, each palm a bed of static black water.

Mottled geode bore a hollowed
tableau of quartz arranged
as within a crèche. If

I found one now,
I might just hold it,
trade emblem

for firm, blank weight. Or:
release my hand over the eroding sand.

ORACIÓNES: FORGOTTEN PRAYERS

I.

God works all things for The Good, the nurse
will say holding Grandmother's hand.
The nurse does not know

she sat tongue-tied for two weeks,
lost in failing verses. Overnight
the lines hid like snakes in watery caves;

illness, unexplainable, came
and rendered illegible the whole.
What the nurse does know:

that Grandmother comprehends
as well as before, but without the words to hold
all movement in place she cannot say
whether or how it is good.

II.

On a house call, the nurse will ask
if she reads her Bible.

Grandmother will shake her head, no.
She will shake her head

when she forgets things too,
and squint, an attempt to slow blink

them back (as cats do to tell their humans, *Sorry*
or *I am tame for you*); and if she cannot,

she'll close her eyes. *What book?*
What need to read the words I know.

III.

Her hand is a full jar of honey; miel
also in mouth, same as her Indio father, father

of instruction in memorized cycles of blessings
and celestial pleas. Her father, she says to me

in her kitchen, loved her more
than anyone. She was his Jesusita, a name

she doesn't use anymore. Jesusita, her father,
called from his dying nights, and she flew

to him in her other country;
she met his petition, her hand holding his at last

rites. Jesusita returned—she tells me this,
when his inheritance

rises again to her tongue; father, Father,
prayer, oración; Dios te bendiga. Gods bless you.

FAITH IS THE LAND YOU'LL TRAVEL

Trek over Asiatic passages long melted back
into the cold ocean. Follow a southern trail, almonds
to avocados, sequoias to cacti. Or, ride north by horse
stopping mission by mission by red clay mission. Palms

and cupped fingers spill over with salt water, rip currents
hold deep—and what was loved slips beyond reach.
Press your ear to the rattle underfoot. Burning
mountains rain in ash. The nostril burns with sulfuric gases

bursting in forest hot spring pits. Fall into the split
rift of moving plates. Try to touch the serpent-border
sliding and slinking along hot desert sands. Look and
be comforted in the bright eye of a wildfire closing in,

comfort in the blind force that overwhelms. It'll set
its rings upon your charred, glistering heart but let you leave.

PART II

"My landscape is a hand with no lines,
The roads bunched to a knot,
The knot myself,

Myself the rose you achieve—"

— *"Childless Woman,"* Sylvia Plath

He split the rocks in the wilderness
And gave them abundant drink like the ocean depths....
They said, "Can God prepare a table in the wilderness?

— Psalm 78:15,19

WHO KNOWS WHY
"All shall be well, and all shall be well and all manner of thing shall be well"
—Julian of Norwich

I.

On those camp-light nights, girls on pilgrimage, our tent flaps
flip and billow, bonfires flicker, our maternal guardian, grand-
mother called Lady, begins *the* tale—truest terror she can
conjure—of La Llorona's curse. One-hundred and one nights

would be filled with this wandering woman and we'd listen;
follow her shivering, chest deep and holding—o boy,
o girl—under water her children. They sank like rocks
lost to the river. As shadows, we found it easy to trace

Lady's voice deep into the fulcrum past of that woman: Sisters,
cousins, aunts, mamas, every girl born through our Lady, rapt
breath, watched the flames, pictured for ourselves the half-formed
and placeless court-room, heard the accounting that never

added up, glimpsed our own unseeable godhead
mete out her fate, for all the nights behind and before us.

II.

Sliver of sun, slit to the city locked
off from an anchor-hold cell; in living
burial, Julian reached
beyond unknowing, composed
her cosmic papers, called Christ,
the "Moder," and wrote Her Blood

from Friday's wounds was the pierced
heart of separation, a wretched blood-
bath like any other birth.

III.

La Llorona, not yet howling ghost; a howling
Eve in God's night court, she is all
but naked. She lies, of course:
they are home, happy, fine.

She must know he knows
"too many babies, too many
mouths." Her own young bones
stretched to the last centimeter

of breaking. Grave-faced, I note
not unkind are the murderess's eyes—
those asked to weep each long
night for centuries more;

they drift to-and-fro as if
to float the question, Does
God know just
how the body betrays?

IV.

Perhaps, because Moses once went down the river,
and most egg and sperm meetings will self-destruct,

perhaps because sacrifice often, God knows,
begins with the children. Yes,

perhaps because of this, what sinks the girl in the end were not
wet hands but the course of her lie. A lie she must
retrace each moonrise.

V.

Moder,   Moder,   have you not known bitter water or sought
                      baptism also in an eternal rest? Moder:
                      what trial and crime have you refused

                      likewise to confess? You too once wept.
                      So do as you have done before among
                      the deserted, spread your skirt over the
exposed;

                      soak up the blood; soothsay, it's only
                      a tale we told our girls, who knows why; a
fable

                      whose ending you will revise.

SEA LESSONS

A ridge rolled across the sea's wide plane,
collapsed in thrashing, whitewater. Already rib-deep,

we dove into the turbulent pit. My breath and fear
held tight by its spinning. Hard arms batting, we drove

deeper and farther, until Mother and child-I
moved like eels over a smooth sand belly, the calm

layer that always lurks just lower than one wants
to push. We rose again beyond

the breaks and the surf's biggest waves, salt water
spilt in coughs from my pinched lips; I spit away

the metallic stew of fish scales and saline
though I could not untaste that filmy throat-

cling of life's origins. We buoyed without time
calling and let salt do its work, doubled

our height; our bodies drifted over quiet, rippled
rows. We floated, apart, we floated. Mother's hair

slung out like seaweed strands;
my legs transformed, slick fins in water.

LISTENING TO GHOSTS

The ghost who lived with my grandparents
took hot showers, ran down hallways,
even napped beside my grandmother.
Shut up. Don't say anything, she'd hush.
Then lean near me and tell how the mattress
sank and its breath swept behind her neck. Later,
when my grandmother became a widow,
she left that house and kept cautioning her grandkids
to *love God and go to sleep* before midnight:
for after nightfall, a cursed woman would steal
wide-awake children. Perhaps it is because of this
early belief, I can't shake the sense that once
my mother saved me when a locked pantry's high
latch shut me in with a clack. Shuddering
she grabbed me and fled the "For Rent"
apartment. Left the front door ajar, same
as our arrival. For two decades, I lived five blocks
from there and we never passed that street again.
My grandfather, too, I only truly knew as ghost
conjured in final legend. For a week, after he died,
he dimmed my mother's doorway,
wanting to say, before his shadow fled,
Take care of your mother. I tell my mother I doubt
our family fables, irrational epimythium
appending the past. Specters bred
as much in the bone as any shadow. I cannot
escape the shape of them. Even now,
I'm followed in thought by the original
ghost. It would whistle at my aunt
changing in the guestroom—a pig for a ghost.
I'm cast into the past, in their house and its wounds.
Whose unresolved memory is it
when I tell you there was an actual pig too,
the beloved pet of an aunt? It expired

one too-hot day during its leashed-walk uphill.
I have no other tether or moral for this but to say,
they ate the pig, threw a party, my aunt cried. Do I then
dare deny these voices when even as I write
no other words come but *Take Care, Love
God, Don't Say Anything.*

ASH WEDNESDAY

Father rubs oil and ash
balm on the brow
presses down his thumb,
sloughing off skin
in the now charred
glistening furrows.

> *Remember, O man,*
> *you are dust.*

For where else
to wear another's death,
but on the body, on the skin
which returns
to its origins, turns
back to dust
with each touch? Better:

rewrite us.
Person by person, traced
and collected in a tincture of sweat.
At the arched door, say *go child,*
live as both and all
and all and all.

GRAPE DAY FESTIVAL
—Escondido, California

In the schoolhouse museum, I see them: ladies in long dresses
lean on wagons for snapshots early in the last century. A full-faced
girl-queen, satin ribbon across her chest, reaches
down to hand festival-goers clusters of round,
fat Muscats. Dark, sweet, and heavy, the fruit
heaps over baskets and generous arms. On a field trip,

only street names etched on the corners of old photos
call up the familiar. I strolled Broadway and, like them,
crossed my town's spacious Grand Avenue.
I longed to enter their grainy storefronts, put
my feet to the unpaved streets. I would taste the grapes
even if too bitter and thick-skinned.

I want to belong to history and trust beyond what the tinplate
frames have caught. Despite the uniform faces
and roads caught in monochrome, ones like me exist
there, billowing bloused and field-booted. They're preserved,
beyond sight, in the infinitesimal touch of finger-prints
pressed to the opaque film of the fruit, their human
oils wed to it, bonded to the many small globes.

God, you hate nothing you have made. I will
lock-up little luxuries for forty days, mainstay
of ritual devotion. No milk, no butter, no
cheese for my vow of temporary kindness to
mammalian mothers. I'll live a season as if
their lives mean as much as the dribble
of cream in hot coffee. I've always liked the porcelain
figurine of Jesus as shepherd
on my grandmother's mantle. We don't share
a faith but she accepts low stakes Episcopalianism
because she says, like Catholics we "love Mary"
and Jesus as a baby, meek as a lamb. At the rails, I kneel

and bow to take up the rouge of loss. Last year's
burnt and anointed palms paint my brow
in the terror of the full grown body. The ash
becomes my face to show how sorry
I am for the seasons I won't care. Would God
hate that or hate how soon

I forget? He should. Two steps back into the great
stone narthex, before I even reach my coat,
I swipe my crossed brow. My hand, a palm
smearing palms. I double-cross it all. Each year
I go back because I would like to settle on whether
to be golden and terrible and brief as ash, or else
just good and enduring. I am here as one at the breach,
re-smudged before I think to choose.

TO WHICH WE RETURN

I take the pulse of the moon in hand
and speak of the sea:

I skim the tide's silvered
water in a sand-sunk bottle. Holding it,
the mercurial skin moils and rises,
licks the neck I seal at the lip. I'll bear

away the message, though I
a poor conduit, hold the sea
to my ear and hear only my own
breath above mist and sand.

The gray water clatters
and the lunar light of Earth's satellite
draws me in. I'll raise my glass
when someone asks, *place of origin?*

SAN DIEGO SUNDAYS

Longboards mark shore slopes
like the first beams set

down for crosses: A woman turns
up the beach. She's long,

wet-locked and gaunt-
muscled. Her wetsuit

folds like a second body
slumped at her waist. She holds

her board tucked by the arm, strides
carefree to her Calvary—

weighted but without
suffering. Under her arm,

sand chafes and sifts. Under
her feet, tectonic ridges

rift. Under every pleasure,
threat.

OPEN ARMED

Twice one flight, airport security
wrenches my arms. A stranger
searches my shoulder blades. Hands move
down my body from pits to hips, even part
my heart, prayer-pressed together they slice
sternum to the firm ribbing
under each breast. I was once a child

feeling out theology. My tight young back lifted
my shoulders, extended each elbow and led
the fingers articulate as a fresco. The warm
dust of legend glowed in my arms: I knew
how His heart felt open, how uncommon

but easy to try Him. These days, I am dark
as Christ and nearing his age, my body
pinioned before the look-away masses. *Oh*, girl
how the vinegar tastes to know now
you should have practiced the thief's part.

SURVIVAL

I fear the inflamed mosquito bite, the rustle of rodents,
the carriers of plagues and hantavirus. I shudder at swamp
foot sores, frostbit nose tips, bacterial invaders (water of dysentery,
many-colored fevers, brain malaria). Regardless, I consume survival
shows with a hunger to match that couple who couldn't
make fire and all but starved on scant sea snails and too little
water. I crave some elemental dread to obscure our
book of common burdens, the ones we rehearse before bed
and on rising, the ones we each to our mothers avoid
sharing because...well, where to begin? So, I weep when they weep
and they say, *The gnats are in my eyes*, or, *I dream of food*;
I whoop, when they whoop, at the rabid deer carcass
they'll skin for warmth and twist its sinews to a fire-
starter. Surviving is harder than living—I've watched
thorn-ripped skin grow thin on bones still marching.

HEAVENLY BODIES

I have never been more beautiful
than in the ease of beach towel borders.
Too sun-sapped to call up self-consciousness.
Rest enters at the skin. No other ground
woos like this. In my present distance,
I can almost find myself there
again. Metallic sunscreen burnishes
rows of exposed backs and long
sweat-swabbed legs. Skin hums as if under
magnetic pulsing. They float, half-buried,
ultraviolet beacons, bodies of light.
As thought, they're out there always—
radiant and burning away.

FAMILY MEDICINE

Rosemary balms wounds and works
as a germicide. Honey quells coughs. Lemon cuts

phlegm. When suffering,
take refuge with the good herb:

yerbabuena of the backyard garden,
unstoppable spreading. We gathered

the mint to simmer in an open pot,
made it our tea with rings of citrus rind

and lemongrass cut from outside next to
the spigot. According to the collected wisdom, some

use yerbabuena for stomachaches, for gout.
Yerbabuena for headaches, sore gums,

pleurisy, rheumatism, hirsutism, pneumonia, nausea, birth
pains. Sedative, stimulant, antiseptic, anesthetic,

diuretic. Yes, yerbabuena, the anodyne applied to burns,
the febrifuge ingested for boiling skin.

Pimples pass away. Poison ivy doesn't itch.
Insomnia closes its eyes. Yerbabuena, cure of colic,

hiccups, and heart palpitation, herb of aphrodisiac,
breath freshener, insect repellent. Subsume each

malady in its perfume. Find healing
that smells like spearmint, tastes like the paste

mama clotted on the flesh's first tear.

TO SEED

I cannot see the mountain for the trees,
neither forest nor waterline. How can I know
what comes past the long-needled pine?

My lover proposes we need a child. Why?
Already, we hear a wailing across the night.
I cannot see the mountain for the trees.

We drink on weekdays, free and glad.
I want what we cannot have.
What comes past the long-needled pine?

My mistake is overthinking. Don't most
just wake up one day their body too large?
I cannot see the mountain nor its trees.

My brooding fills forests of the mind.
I could live decades circling, no need for all
that comes past the long-needled pine.

We wake another day. Find if we
know anything here will grow.
I cannot see. Mountains. Trees.
What comes past the long need and pine.

MOTHER, GRANDMOTHER, DAUGHTER

Mother would be Mary and Martha
in one. She would foot wash, shave the hard
heeled skin into a warm tub, a little throne

and basin placed at grandmother's feet, the television
swirling with Don Francisco. She wrapped
a warm towel around those age-spotted

brown ankles, applied red polish to the just buffed
and scrubbed toes of the eighty year old.
When I was less than one, she cut my nails

and blood like a ladybug bloomed
on my mis-clipped toe and she wept
for nascent failures. I'm told

I suckled my wound and wailed with her
too. Together we cried for all the ways
this tender work was and was not enough.

LITURGY

I.

Beside the garbage cans
where no one goes
on purpose,

the unkempt lawn grows
weed-hearty. The hill
breezes in star thistle

clumping on patch-grass
dirt, dandelions
sway in stages of dispersion.

On a warm, clear
day—for how many years
just like this—I

carry these bags.
The roof-sliced light
marks

half this body and puffed
up in familiar ceremony
something in me stirs,

that earthbound
invocation, saying: Un-weed
me, sun. Un-weed me.

II.

What is the word for
the fixed core
of the mutable?

III.

What a neighbor wrote in public:

there used to be just the right
amount of Mexicans. Now they are

everywhere

I turn.

Imagine ten years, fifteen ...

Imagine how deep
that root.

ROUGH FIRE REDWOODS

Last time I stood under the sequoias,
a teenage philosopher, I wanted to live holy
and humble, bow under the great
vastness of a God and all his tall

makings. They say, in such places to pray
one never comes down from the mountain.
Yet now the mountains ignite. Camps of my youth,
where I sang of the *Refiner's fire*,

have turned to char. Totems of old, more ancient
than Jesus, send smoke trails to space
even the naked eye of God might see.
The angels of the grand cathedral splay

their flamed branches. I want to preserve
that apex of one-time hope. I yearn
to rest my back in an evening's cool bed,
search again the sky lights of bright stars, all framed

by those immense aged heads. But down
from mountains many years, I learned,
not even holiness saves them.

RED TIDE, ORANGE COUNTY

Teens drift down from the Wright-
modeled home set above the beach—their groping
conversations founder and sink
amidst over-precise lines. They seek night

in silent procession, to shoreline shadows
where top-heavy rock formations balance
in the not-too-deep. Across the moon-mirrored
 ocean blazes the unexpected: algae-blooming

waves fracture in a fury of phosphorescent light.
Side by side, youth marvel. Almost-touching
fingers mingle in the flash-studded darkness. How soon
do they dare disappear, leave the cotton on land,

wade, then run in. Roving. Spinning. Each slick,
wet limb becomes a night-flare struck in water.
Fluorescent beacons just formed at ignition, they shimmer
and smolder, are polished in the electric waters.

Whoever they were, whatever mind or heart or meat,
it's melted into background: sand and glass. These,
who on retaking land, bring the sea
ashore. Moon touched faces carry the flame.

SEEN AND UNSEEN IN LAGUNA

A starfish
withers in one dry tide pool

among mosaics of full silver pools:
Push a hand into the dark waters

between the split rocks to find
a living relation; pebbled

hump and hard arms
contrast the yielding underbelly

sucking and clinging
against the unknown thrall.

KINGDOM COME, FULLERTON

We arrived to gilt mirrors worn to tin. The foyer carpet faded
red-orange where the sun had scrubbed thousands of days.
The rented home ill-wore its old frame—vaulted ceilings
streamed light over the curled and split floors where water

seeped up from hair-thin concrete cracks. This island
suburb built on an expected coming—the meeting of tracts
that never took place—left us to parking lots and industrial
neighbors. At night, a sky reign of fireworks and shooting stars,

unnatural but no less bright, fell upon us from the Magic
Kingdom just down the road. Our complaints
diffused into its artificial fog. The luminous blues

and swirling pinks shaded each surface through the patio
glass and entered the mind. Even years on, I see us
best in those punctures of awe and light.

ORACIÓNES: GRANDMOTHER'S BENEDICTION

In the presence of these words, her love for God
tumbles from her lips, an unbidden incantation.
She sends me on my way in a prayer:

verses, in faith, I cannot fluently translate.
But like sensing the day's heat by feet in sand, I feel,
in the presence of these words, her love. For God's

orations now come to her on days resembling
past days. She invokes benedictions, the best ones
she sends me on my way with. A prayer

spread like a net across the muscle of her mind,
litany composed in synaptic fibers woven over and
in the presence of these words. Here, love for God

stitches itself to the edge of memory's wrinkled
tributaries carrying lost children, a salt city, even me, as
she sends me on my way in a prayer.

Yes, by the tissue of memorized blessings, in Spanish
cadence, in eighty years recited by heart,
in the presence of these words: her love for God.
She sends me on my way in a prayer.

NORTH COUNTY CULTIVATION

1920s: Would you believe
for the eighteenth annual Grape
Day Festival, the day's Queen
sailed down Grand Avenue,
a waving Cleopatra
riding an elaborate Egyptian float?
I know the feeling: A swarm
of teen girls, we rode
bicycles down the same streets,
laughing and waving,
circling the park's decorative vines.

1960s: Orange groves
spread across the valley. The largest
citrus packer under one roof
closed for good. And, still,
every backyard, tight corner,
bears an orange tree, lemon tree,
hard tang tree. My friend and I
would ride in the raised
bucket of her parents' tractor
through acres of grapefruit
orchard—their blossoms swirled
and scented the air.

Now: The avocado capital of the country
offers a creamy belly. Neighbors
leave at cross-corners bags
labeled, "Free to good home."
Sometimes in the mix, a gem,
the delicate-skinned, Fuerte. Not
good for shipping but for eating.

Each crop bends toward the abundant
and sweet meat that follows.
We scoop from the rind
whatever turns tender, comes next.

THE GARDENS

Anywhere in Georgia is better than anywhere
in Mexico, a farmer of the American South

reasons on immigration news.
       In Mexico City, architects raise vertical gardens

along skyscrapers to catch carbon in the alchemy
which blooms tropical flowers in the clouds. Look up

and see the bouquets burst from steel. In Mexico City,
young engineers make plans for uprooting

highways to uncover lanes and riverbeds
tamped down in modern time. The transplanted

roads will leave dusty tributaries to fill
once more with coursing water. In Mexico City,

if there is somewhere landscapers
are moving, it is beyond our fathoming.

OUR FATHER

The swing rode diagonal at any speed, made our knees
knock against the rusted pole. Ungrounded,
the set's angled legs drew up, high and hard,
as we heaved forward. My chin bears a cross
scar of body, soul, seat, rope and bars
driven headlong into red dust. Excavate
a landfill of Father's constructions: beside
the unearthed swing rests a windowless
playhouse. Here, a sheet-metal bracelet, so tight
its soldering pinched my veins, my name etched
in/delicate curlicues on the underside. There,
a ladder of splintered planks downed
from where the tree-fort would have been
had it been. His hands, gnarled and calloused,
began each one for me. Their shade suggests
the hue of sweat-formed rust. They shape
a kingdom of power and glory
and imperfect love. Amen, amen.

GRANDMOTHER'S TONGUE: INHERITANCE

Old and short and brown, she walks
the same route as those in cars
and with heavy grocery bags gripped in her fists.
She puts back the onion,
not on sale after all. She's rich beyond
landowning dreams and not telling.
Within the fluorescent scene of a superstore,
Grandmother and I shop for shirt cloth.
She asks a fabric cutter, *Es like this blue, pero, more strong.*
The request reaches a woman turning away; she huffsighs, says,
Hold it. I need a translator. I don't speak that language.
Stunned, I retreat commiserating,
Can you believe—but beside me, she saunters,
arms over the bar of her cart. *Some people's no
happy,* she says coolly, like she's spitting sunflower seeds,
then offers me a sly grin that becomes a cackle. It rises
like song, and we plow on. We move
through wide sliding doors that part
just for us—two little Mexicans, inheriting
the earth. If the lion and the lamb
rest together, they are both sides of
her tongue. A woman like this,
she's learned to speak without saying,
to release without giving in. Later that night,
she'll guide my hand to the stove's fire and
show me how to blister the skin off a pepper
and not get burned.

BIRDS OF PARADISE

It's Escondido *escondido* as the whole old landscape has
been reshaped. I pass my childhood yard, extinct: a hill

filled and flattened, a single-grass lawn unfurled
where once, a sparse thorned bush

bore aphids on its brown-singed cups. Cocooning
caterpillars laced twigs suspended on kitchen jars. Roly-poly

bodies collected in curled heaps at the fence. Sure, this place
holds no capacity to look back to me, any more than a split

earthworm slinking away from its cleaved twin or
a snail shell can tell of the slug's wet tenderness.

Yet, who wouldn't want the earth to attest
to the plots erased with us? I'll tell my part: I was

a young brown body born each afternoon from the ground,
arms shaped by clover and grass. Blade by blade

I uncovered ladybugs and let their orange blood
streak my hands. I wore the head of the broken Queen

of Flowers, strelitzia, gathered from the dust. I nosed around
in the earthy must of private kingdoms. I've lain

face to the sun, ears filling with the buzz and hiss
and hum of things barely seen. Each day

a day in solitude except the thrum of battles won
by the edges of super-colony ant empires conquering

five continents to meet at my door and war across this particular
street. A hundred thousand dead would lie by me, but only I arose.

I know what happened here, the skin ripping ridges on never-to-
fruit palm tree fronds, the silk of worms, the dirt-filled

nails clawing gravel to unbury armored insect bodies,
scraping, along the way, shattered bones and fool's gold aplenty.

TO EXPLAIN CALIFORNIA GEOGRAPHY

I sign the cross, a compass over my body:
My open hand lifts to heavenly Los

Angeles, drops south near my belly,
San Diegan in origin. I sweep west-east

across my chest from Orange County's seaside
carnal cities, then over the divide of Santa Ana

Mountains toward the Inland,
where I end this empire; in the interior—

paused, my hand marks
where desert meets valley in the high,

hard heat that yields, year after year,
a landscape of wine, vineyards of dark fruit.

NOTES

The character of Queen Calafia derives from early modern Spanish chivalric romance *Las Sergas de Esplandián* by Garci Rodríguez de Montalvo. It is a continuation of his chivalric cycle that begins with *Amadís de Gaula*. In Montalvo's telling, Queen Calafia ruled over a nation of dark-skinned warrior women on a mythical island called "California." The quotation was translated by D. Polk.

"Yerbabuena" includes found language from the "Mint" entry in the book, *Chicano Folk Medicine from Los Angeles, California*.

ACKNOWLEDGEMENTS

Thank you to the journals and literary organizations where versions of these poems first appeared: "Birds of Paradise," *Hayden's Ferry Review*. "Listening to Ghosts," *Nimrod International Journal*. "Santa Monica" and "Hominy," *Crab Orchard Review*. "Labor," *Nashville Review*. "Countrymen," *The Acentos Review*. "Grandmother's Tongue: Inheritance" and "To Explain California Geography," *Christianity and Literature*. "Santa Ana," as winner of the Leonard Steinberg Contest. "Rendered Miracles," (as "Hortense Talks to Her Reflection in the Window"), *The Saint Ann's Review*.

My deepest gratitude to Noemi Press and each individual who touched this book and helped usher it into the world. Thank you to Carmen Giménez Smith for your leadership and significant support of my work. Thank you to Suzi Garcia, Anthony Cody, and Mirna Palacio Ornelas for all your editorial guidance. You each extended such generosity of time, enthusiasm, and a willingness to push me to make better art. My thanks to Sarah Gzemski and Natalie Eilbert for the care in layout of the book and cover design.

I am indebted to my time learning with Robin Becker and Julia Spicher Kasdorf. This book began in their classes. To Robin, my particular thanks for the joy and perseverance you inspire in me as I make poetry my life. To Julia, my appreciation for showing the way in writing what is closest to my core.

To Chris Davidson, when I stepped into your workshop the world of poetry sprang opened to me. To Virginia Doland, my heartfelt thanks for nurturing my love of literature and hard questions.

To Juliette Diggs De Soto, my first poetry reader and kindred friend, thank you for every call, message and day. To Jarod Roselló and Angie Roselló, thank you for your friendship; it makes me a more thoughtful person and writer.

Thank you familia for your encouragement. To my mother, Sylvia Magaña, I am grateful for being witness to your power. To my sisters, Christina and Yvonne, thank you for the days of sun and play. To my father, Paul Huizar, thank you for showing me imagination. To all my grandmothers, aunts, uncles and cousins, our days around the table are gifts to me.

To Gabriel Ford, my spouse, my light: your avid support has made this book possible. You have spurred on my writing life and have been a constant and generous reader of these poems. Thank you for the multitude ways you share in this work with me.

BIOGRAPHY

Leah Huizar is a Mexican-American writer originally from Southern California. She holds an MFA from Penn State University. Her writing and research interests center on the cultural and historic landscape of the west coast. *Inland Empire* is her first poetry collection. She can be found online at leahhuizar.com.